HOW DO PLANTS GET FOOD?

First Steck-Vaughn Edition 1992

Copyright © 1989 American Teacher Publications

Published by Steck-Vaughn Company

Library of Congress number: 89-3577

Library of Congress Cataloging in Publication Data.

Goldish, Meish.
　How do plants get food? / Meish Goldish; illustrated by Tom Powers.

　(Real readers)
　Summary: Explains, in simple terms, how plants make food.
　1. Photosynthesis—Juvenile literature. [1. Photosynthesis.] I. Powers, Tom (Tom J.), ill. II. Title III. Series.
　QK882.G64　1989　581.1'3342—dc19　　　　　　　　　　　　　　89-3577

ISBN 0-8172-3507-8　hardcover library binding

ISBN 0-8114-6708-2　softcover binding

　　4 5 6 7 8 9 0　96 95 94 93 92

How Do Plants Get Food?

by Meish Goldish
illustrated by Tom Powers

RSVP
RAINTREE
STECK-VAUGHN
P U B L I S H E R S
The Steck-Vaughn Company

Austin, Texas

You need food. Your pets need food.
Plants need food, too.

Here are the parts of a plant.

It has leaves.

It has a stem.

It has roots.

leaves

stem

roots

A green plant has to make the food it needs to grow. A green plant needs air, water, and light to make food.

A green plant takes in air, water, and light.

A plant takes in air through its leaves.

The leaves have lots of little holes. The holes are too little for you to see. But the plant takes in air through the little holes in its leaves.

air

air hole

A plant takes in water through its roots.

The roots are in the soil. The soil has water in it. The roots take in the water. Then the water goes up through the stem to the leaves.

water

Now air and water are in the leaves. But the plant needs light, too. The plant needs light so that the air and water can join to make food.

Light hits the green leaves. When the light hits the green leaves, the air and water can join. Now the plant will have the food it needs.

light

What if a green plant does not get water?

If it does not get water, the plant can't make food. The plant will die.

light

air

What if a green plant does not get light?

If it does not get light, the plant can't make food. The plant will die.

You can help your plants to grow. Give your plants water. Put your plants in the light.

You can't see air, but it is there! You don't have to help plants get air.

When the light hits the green leaves, the air and the water will join to make food. The plants will grow and GROW and GROW.

Sharing the Joy of Reading

Beginning readers enjoy reading books on their own. Reading a book is a worthwhile activity in and of itself for a young reader. However, a child's reading can be even more rewarding if it is shared. This sharing can enhance your child's appreciation—both of the book and of his or her own abilities.

Now that your child has read **How Plants Get Food**, you can help extend your child's reading experience by encouraging him or her to:

- Retell the story or key concepts presented in this story in his or her own words. The retelling can be oral or written.

- Create a picture of a favorite character, event, or concept from this book.

- Express his or her own ideas and feelings about the subject of this book and other things he or she might want to know about this subject.

Here is an activity that you can do together to help extend your child's appreciation of this book: Your child has read that water goes up through a green plant's roots, through the stem, and into the leaves. You can do an experiment that shows that this does happen. You'll need a fresh stalk of celery with leaves attached, some blue or red food coloring, and a glass of water. Add a few drops of food coloring to the water. Then ask your child to place the celery in the glass of water, leaves up. Wait a few hours. The coloring will have made its way up the stem and into the leaves. If you slice the celery you will see colored tubes in the plant that carry water up to the leaves.